D1713029

BUENOS AIRES

MARION MORRISON

WORLD ALMANAC® LIBRARY

Please visit our web site at: www.worldalmanaclibrary.com
For a free color catalog describing World Almanac® Library's list of high-quality books and multimedia programs, call 1-800-848-2928 (USA) or 1-800 387-3178 (Canada). World Almanac® Library's fax: (414) 332-3567.

Library of Congress Cataloging-in-Publication Data

Morrison, Marion.
    Buenos Aires / by Marion Morrison.
        p. cm. — (Great cities of the world)
    Includes bibliographical references and index.
    ISBN 0-8368-5044-0 (lib.bdg.)
    ISBN 0-8368-5204-4 (softcover)
    1. Buenos Aires (Argentina)—Juvenile literature. I. Title. II. Series.
    F3001.M677   2005
    982'.11—dc22   2004057145

First published in 2005 by
World Almanac® Library
330 West Olive Street, Suite 100
Milwaukee, WI 53212 USA

Copyright © 2005 by World Almanac® Library.

Produced by Discovery Books
Editors: Valerie Weber and Kathryn Walker
Series designers: Laurie Shock, Keith Williams
Designer and page production: Keith Williams
Photo researcher: Rachel Tisdale
Diagrams: Keith Williams
Maps: Stefan Chabluk
World Almanac® Library editorial direction: Mark J. Sachner
World Almanac® Library editor: Gini Holland
World Almanac® Library art direction: Tammy West
World Almanac® Library graphic design: Scott M. Krall
World Almanac® Library production: Jessica Morris

Photo credits: Getty Images/AFP/Ho: p. 15; Getty Images/Chad Ehlers: cover and title page; Getty Images/Keystone: p. 14; James Davis Travel: pp. 7, 33; South American Pictures: pp. 9, 10; South American Pictures/Jason P. Howe: p. 16; South American Pictures/Tony Morrison: pp. 8, 13, 18, 19, 20, 23, 25, 34, 37, 43; South American Pictures/Frank Nowikowski: pp. 27, 32, 39, 41; South American Pictures/Chris Sharp: pp. 29, 30; Still Pictures/Mark Edwards: p. 24; Still Pictures/Ron Giling: pp. 21, 36; Trip/Art Directors & Trip: pp. 11, 26.

Cover caption: Claimed to be the world's widest avenue, Avenida 9 de Julio is 425 feet (130 meters) wide and has sixteen lanes of traffic.

Printed in Canada

1 2 3 4 5 6 7 8 9 09 08 07 06 05

Contents

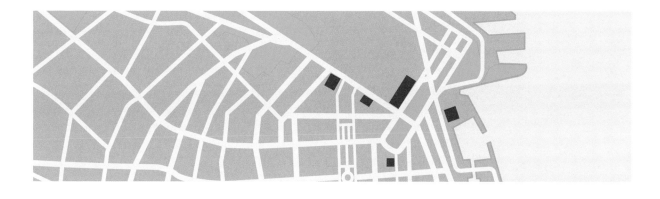

Introduction

The capital of Argentina, Buenos Aires is the third largest city in South America. It lies on the southern shore of the Río de la Plata (Plate River) estuary, formed where the Paraná and Uruguay Rivers meet. Montevideo, the capital of Uruguay, is on the northern shore.

Forty-eight barrios, or neighborhoods, make up the city of Buenos Aires. The city

◄ *The Avenida 9 de Julio runs from north to south between the barrios of San Telmo and Retiro.*

itself is bordered by the Plate River, the Riachuelo River, and the Avenida (Avenue) General Paz and covers some 77 square miles (200 square kilometers). It is part of metropolitan, or greater, Buenos Aires, which, with nineteen outer suburbs, extends over a vast area of 1,497 square miles (3,877 sq km).

Pampas, or grasslands, surround greater Buenos Aires to the west and south. Flat, open, and treeless as far as the eye can see, the pampas are home to herds of cattle. Livestock has been the basis of Argentina's economy since Spanish settlers introduced cattle in the sixteenth century. In fact, Buenos Aires developed because of its importance as a port for shipping beef; by the eighteenth century, it was one of the principal cities of colonial South America.

Today, some 12 million people, almost half of Argentina's population, lives in greater Buenos Aires. Of these, 3 million live in the city. They are known as *porteños*, or "people of the port."

Porteños, The People of Buenos Aires

There are two things about which many porteños are especially passionate: soccer and tango. Almost half, and the best, of all Argentina's soccer clubs are based in Buenos

"It seems to me a tale that Buenos Aires ever began; I consider it as eternal as water and air."

— Jorge Luis Borges, in his 1929 poem, "The Mythical Foundation of Buenos Aires."

CITY FACTS

Buenos Aires
Capital of Argentina

Founded: 1536

Area (City): 77 square miles (200 square kilometers)

Area (Metropolitan): 1,497 square miles (3,877 square kilometers)

Population (City): 2.8 million

Population (Metropolitan): 12 million

Population Density (city): 36,363 per sq m (14,000 per sq km); (metropolitan) 8,016 per sq m (3,095 per sq km)

Aires. Rowdy and emotional, matches can bring the city streets to a standstill. For porteños, to tango is to forget their troubles, and tango is everywhere. Singers and dancers feature in large murals on buildings and in paintings in the subway. Dancing couples entertain crowds in market places and parks.

Working-class porteños also still remember with great affection their heroine, Eva Perón, who became known worldwide through the musical *Evita*. Graffiti, mementos on sale, and flowers at her grave are daily reminders of Argentina's First Lady, who died in 1952.

Metropolitan Area

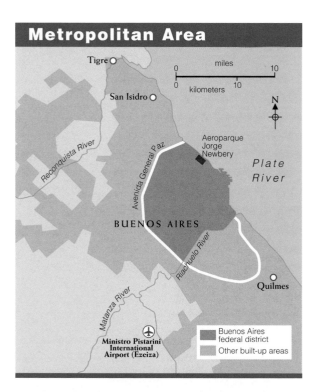

City Center

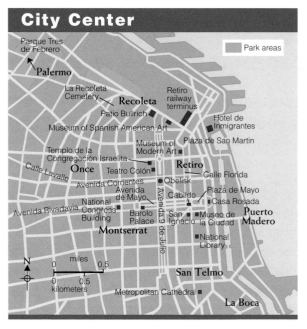

Climate

Since it is south of the equator, Buenos Aires' seasons are the opposite of those in northern countries. During the summer months of December to February, the climate can be hot and humid, with temperatures rising to 95° Fahrenheit (35° Celsius). The winter months of June to August can also be humid but are milder, with temperatures averaging 52° Fahrenheit (11° C). An occasional strong wind known as the pampero *sweeps in from the* pampas. *Rainfall is moderate, about 45 inches (114 centimeters) during the year, and frosts can occur between May and September. It snowed here only twice in the twentieth century, in 1918 and 1955.*

The Streets of Buenos Aires

The heart of Buenos Aires is the Plaza de Mayo in the old part of the city, close to the waterfront. Traditionally, people gather in this main square for important events or to hold protests. Built between 1874 and 1882, the presidential palace, called the Casa Rosada, or Pink House, covers one side of the plaza. Other principal buildings are the Metropolitan Cathedral, the city's legislative and government buildings, and the Cabildo, or city hall.

The broad Avenida de Mayo, 1 mile (1.6 kilometers) long, links the Casa Rosada to the National Congress Building. Avenida 9 de Julio, one of the world's widest streets, crosses the Avenida de Mayo. The 220-foot (67-meter) high Obelisko (obelisk), built in the 1930s to commemorate the four hundredth anniversary of the city's founding, dominates Avenida 9 de Julio. Amazingly, 157 workers created the monument in thirty-one days.

Notable Neighborhoods

Nearby are some of the city's most famous streets—Calle Lavalle, Avenida Corrientes, and Calle Florida. Calle Florida is a pedestrian mall lined with shops, tearooms, and bars and stays open until the early hours, ablaze with lights and filled with crowds and noise. The city's financial district, known as La City, is close by. The city's longest street at 25 miles (40 km) long, Avenida Rivadavia, divides the city.

Buenos Aires' most famous residential barrios are also close to the Plaza de Mayo. To the south are the older barrios of the city, such as San Telmo and La Boca. These neighborhoods are traditionally working class, where immigrants, especially Italians, settled. Today, tourists flock to see the brightly painted tin houses and visit the flea markets. To the north stand the newer,

▲ The Casa Rosada stands on the site of an original fort that was built in 1595.

"[The city is] large and I should think one of the most regular in the world. Every street is at right angles to the one it crosses, and the parallel ones being equidistant, the houses are collected into solid squares of equal dimensions, which are called quadras."

—Scientist Charles Darwin, who visited Buenos Aires in 1833.

middle- and upper-class neighborhoods collectively known as the Barrio Norte. Suburbs include those along the Plate River estuary such as San Isidro and Tigre, which is a popular weekend resort. Others, such as Quilmes to the south, are important industrial centers. In the outer suburbs sprawl extensive shantytowns, known as *villas miserias* (miserable houses), where poor immigrants live.

CHAPTER 1

History of Buenos Aires

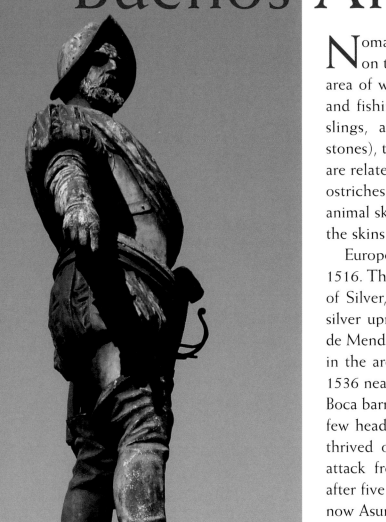

Nomadic Querandí Indians once lived on the open plains of Argentina in the area of what is now Buenos Aires, hunting and fishing. With bows and arrows, darts, slings, and bolas (cords weighted with stones), they caught deer, guanacos, which, are related to llamas, and rheas, which, like ostriches, are flightless birds. They used animal skins as garments and also stretched the skins over poles to make shelters.

Europeans first reached the Plate River in 1516. They called it Río de la Plata, or River of Silver, because they believed there was silver upriver. A Spanish nobleman, Pedro de Mendoza established the first settlement in the area now known as Buenos Aires in 1536 near the Riachuelo River in today's La Boca barrio. Mendoza also brought the first few head of cattle and some horses, which thrived on the pampas. Constantly under attack from the native Querandí Indians, after five years he moved upriver to what is now Asunción, the capital of Paraguay.

The City of Good Airs

It was not until 1580 that Juan de Garay, a soldier and governor of the Río de la Plata provinces, refounded the settlement, which

◄ The Spanish conquistador Juan de Garay was governor of Río de la Plata from 1574 to 1583.

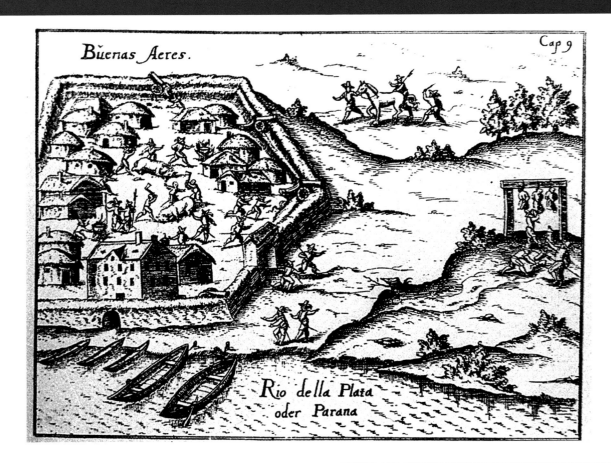

Büenas Aeres.

Cap 9

Rio della Plata
oder Parana

▲ *This sixteenth-century engraving depicts the founding of Buenos Aires and the battle between the conquistadors and the Querandí Indians.*

he named Nuestra Senõra Santa María del Buen Aire (Santa María of the good winds), after the patron saint of sailors. The settlement was divided into *manzanas*, or blocks, and a street grid system developed that is the basis of the old city today. There were no trees or stones on the pampas, so the first buildings were of baked mud bricks.

Within a century of the Spanish arrival, Querandí Indians were apparently extinct. Diseases brought by the Spanish killed most of them, but no one is sure if they all died or if they were later identified as Pampa Indians.

Silver and Smuggling

In the Andes Mountains far west of Buenos Aires, the Spaniards had immense silver mines in the Cerro Rico, or Rich Hill, of Potosí, where they used Indians as slave labor. Spanish rulers had forbidden their colonies throughout South and Central America from trading with any country besides Spain. All of the empire's imports and exports had to pass through Lima, the capital of Peru, which was also ruled by Spain. The silver, therefore, was shipped back to Spain from Lima, but this involved a long and difficult journey. It was actually quicker to smuggle the silver from Potosí downriver to Buenos Aires and across the Atlantic Ocean to Spain.

By 1667, Buenos Aires had about four thousand inhabitants and was still little more than a village. People traded cattle and agricultural produce and supplied beef and animals to Spanish mining towns in Peru and Bolivia.

Ignoring Spain's requirement that exports go through Lima, the people of Buenos Aires survived by smuggling silver and other contraband. Anxious to trade with the colonies, the French, English, and Portuguese took advantage of the Spaniards being on the other side of the continent and encouraged the illegal trade.

As the smuggling trade grew, Buenos Aires became increasingly prosperous. Recognizing its value, in 1776, Spain made it the capital and administrative center of the newly formed Viceroyalty of Río de la Plata, a large area composed of the present-day countries of Argentina, Uruguay, Bolivia, Paraguay, and the north of Chile.

Independence

In 1806 and 1807, the British invaded Buenos Aires. General William Beresford led the first attack and was initially successful—the Spanish viceroy fled, and Beresford became the city's governor. He lasted only forty-five days. General John Whitelocke

▼ *This watercolor, painted in about 1825, shows the market square in what is today the Plaza de Mayo. The arched building is the Cabildo as it originally appeared.*

"Buenos Aires is called a city, but in Germany many villages are larger. . . . In itself Buenos Aires is ugly; it only has three churches, with ours, the worst, found near the center, by the fort. On one side is the Franciscan convent, on the other the attractive cathedral built in lime and bricks and covered in tiles; all the buildings are built with sticks and mud, like swallows' nests."

—German Jesuit Miguel Herre in 1727.

led the second attack with eighty-four hundred soldiers. Not wanting to destroy the city, Whitelocke instructed his men not to use artillery. The soldiers in the streets were easy targets for the locals who poured boiling water and dropped stones on them from rooftops and windows. Whitelocke lost almost three thousand men in nine days.

The porteños' victory over the British gave them a new sense of independence and nationalism. In 1810, two years after the French emperor Napoléon Bonaparte overthrew the Spanish king, Buenos Aires declared its independence from Spain. It was not until 1816, however, that the whole country became independent.

What Kind of Government?

From then until the 1880s, Buenos Aires was at odds with the interior provinces of Argentina. The provinces wanted a federal government with power shared between

The Cabildo

The Cabildo, or Town Hall, on the Plaza de Mayo was constructed in 1751 on the site of the first town hall. It originally spanned the length of the plaza with five great arches on either side, but much of it was torn down to make way for the Avenida de Mayo. It was from this building that Argentineans declared their independence from Spain. Today, a small museum in this building exhibits documents, paintings, arms, medals, and maps relating to that period.

the provinces and a central government as well as protection for local industries and commerce. Buenos Aires, however, favored a stronger central government that was open to international trade and European immigration. From 1829 to 1852, Juan Manuel de Rosas was governor of Buenos Aires. A federalist with no sympathy for the pro-European liberals of the city, at first he had the support of the provinces. Rosas, however, became a strong and ruthless governor who ruled with the help of a secret police and was greatly feared. He put the interests of Buenos Aires above everything else—including the interior provinces and the federalists, who gradually turned against him.

The conflict between the provinces and Buenos Aires was resolved only when Bartolomé Mitre became president in 1862, and Buenos Aires, prospering from taxes levied on imports and exports, dominated the rest of the country. In 1880, the Buenos Aires province and federal capital district was established, and the city was officially recognized as the capital.

The City Changes

In the last decades of the nineteenth century, Buenos Aires was transformed. In the 1880s, General Julio Roca and the army wiped out the last of the Native peoples in the south of the country, and ranchers and farmers took over the land. At the same time, refrigeration and improvements in shipping meant that more meat and other

"One of the first objects that strikes the eye of a stranger on landing, is a water-cart. By this clumsy contrivance, consisting of a butt raised upon a rude cart with two wheels eight feet high, drawn by bullocks, the whole city is supplied with this prime necessary."

—From *The Modern Traveller*, published in 1825, author unknown.

exports could be sent to Europe. Buenos Aires' importance as a port and industrial center increased further with the construction of railroads across the pampas that connected the city to wealthy ranches in the interior.

The city's new wealth inspired a building boom. Many old buildings were torn down to make way for grand mansions and ornate housing that reflected French and Italian design. Great avenues were carved through the city. New neighborhoods, such as Retiro, Palermo, and Recoleta, were created on land reclaimed from the river. Urban improvements included street lighting, gas supplies to many homes and businesses, and better water supplies. Public schools, newspapers, publishing houses, a national bank, and a world-class opera house were also founded.

The greatest impact on the city came with the vast numbers of immigrants who arrived from Europe. Between 1869 and 1914, the population of Buenos Aires grew

The Barolo Palace

Luis Barolo, an Italian immigrant, arrived in Argentina in 1890. He was a successful textile merchant who commissioned the Barolo Palace (pictured left), an extraordinary building on Avenida de Mayo. Dating from 1922, it was designed with references to the Italian poet Dante Alighieri's Divine Comedy *and his vision of heaven and hell. Until the Kavanagh Building was erected in 1936, it was the highest building in Buenos Aires.*

from 177,000 to over 1.2 million. Most came from Italy and Spain. Workers were needed for the industries and to construct the railways. All immigrants were given five days to stay for free at the Hotel de Inmigrantes, which still stands in the North Dock. Most remained in the city, settling in areas like La Boca or around the port. City suburbs also developed as new local train lines and a trolley system connected outer areas to the city center.

The Early Twentieth Century

In May 1910, the people of Buenos Aires celebrated one hundred years of independence with a great march down the Avenida de Mayo. By then, it was the largest and wealthiest city in South America. The working classes were not happy, however; many were immigrants with poorly paid jobs or no jobs at all. Their trade unions, often led by anarchists and communists, threatened the city with bombs, assassinations, and strikes. In January 1919, in one week now known as *la semana trágica,* "the tragic week," a thousand people died during protests.

By the 1930s, international immigration had virtually stopped, due to the worldwide Great Depression, but migrants continued to flow into the city from other parts of Argentina. Housing was in short supply, and the first of the villas miserias, or shantytowns, appeared on the edge of the city.

Political Struggles

Argentina stayed neutral through much of World War II, but its political problems at home did not go away; the military was ready to step in and take over the government at any time. Threatened by the military but supported by a large number of workers and farmers—as evidenced by a huge demonstration by the working masses in the Plaza de Mayo on October 17, 1945— Juan Perón was elected president in 1946.

The military rebelled against Perón in 1955, and civil war followed. The air force bombed Casa Rosada, and three hundred people died in the Plaza de Mayo. In revenge, Peronistas, followers of Perón, burned down many of the city's famous churches, which they felt represented the elite ruling class of Argentina. The military took over the government and put successive generals in power.

After the military takeover, Argentina's political and economic problems got worse.

María Eva Duarte de Perón

Eva Perón (pictured above) *was First Lady of Argentina for only a few years, from 1946 until her death in 1952, but her impact on the country was extraordinary. Born in 1919 to a poor, rural family, at age fifteen she moved to Buenos Aires to become an actress. She did not forget her origins and was very active in gaining the support of the working masses for her husband, Colonel Juan Perón, when he ran for the presidency. As president, he introduced social reforms to help the workers, while she created various organizations and charities to help the poor and fight for women's rights. Eva Perón was not without her critics, however, who accused her of using money from her charities to benefit herself and her family. The upper classes hated her. Her early death from cancer brought Buenos Aires to a standstill, and people still mourn for her today.*

In the 1970s, guerrilla groups plagued Buenos Aires with kidnappings, bombs, and assassinations. A return to power by Juan Perón in 1973 did not help the situation. Perón died the following year and his third wife, Isabelle, took over the presidency. Terrorist activities, strikes, and economic problems increased, and in 1976, the military again seized power. The military regime lasted until 1983, presiding over a period of such repression against opponents—including murder, arrests for political activity, and kidnapping people that were never found again—that it became known as the "Dirty War."

A Return to Democracy

The military also provoked a disastrous conflict with Great Britain when it invaded the British-governed Malvinas, or Falkland Islands, in 1982. After nearly a three-month war with Argentina, Britain retook the islands. In 1983, Argentina returned to democracy with the government of Raúl Alfonsín. President Carlos Menem, elected in 1989, dominated the last years of the century. He tried to control the rising costs of goods and balance the national budget, and he sold nationally-run businesses to private companies. The rapid growth of the population in the last half of the twentieth century, however, severely strained Buenos Aires' ability to provide housing, electricity, water, and other services, and a severe downturn in the economy left many people living in poverty.

▲ *During the inauguration of President Raúl Alfonsín in December 1983, a crowd filled the Plaza de Mayo to celebrate Argentina's return to democracy.*

Menem's presidency ended in 1999 with the election of Fernando de la Rúa, who tried to improve the economic situation by cutting government spending and increasing taxes. His policies led to people protesting in the streets, however, and he was forced to resign in 2001. The situation did not improve under his successor, Eduardo Duhalde. In 2003, Néstor Kirchner became president and helped bring some stability to the economy. The country still faces many problems, with a high number of people unemployed.

CHAPTER 2

People of Buenos Aires

The population of the city of Buenos Aires grew from more than one million in 1914 to almost five million in the 1940s. Today, the metropolitan area's population stands at around twelve million. The most recent trend has been the inflow of *mestizos*, mixed Native American and Spanish people, moving to Buenos Aires from outlying provinces, and other Latin Americans emigrating from across the continent. These arrivals now make up as much as one-third of the total population.

Porteños

Hopeful immigrants flooding into Argentina in the late nineteenth and early twentieth centuries created a hard-working, prosperous society. People landed in Buenos Aires from around the world. Some arrived with just a few dollars in their pockets, and some, like Aristotle Onassis from Greece, went on to become some of the world's wealthiest people.

Most porteños today are descendants of Italian and Spanish immigrants. Their skin is generally lighter than that of many of their Latin neighbors and many have

◀ *The Sunday flea market held in the Plaza Dorrego is very popular with porteños and tourists. Couples dance the tango in the street to entertain the crowds.*

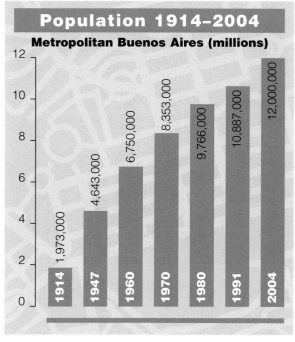

Population 1914–2004
Metropolitan Buenos Aires (millions)

- 1914: 1,973,000
- 1947: 4,643,000
- 1960: 6,750,000
- 1970: 8,353,000
- 1980: 9,766,000
- 1991: 10,887,000
- 2004: 12,000,000

Lunfardo

A regional dialect and distinctive vocabulary known as "Plate River Spanish" heavily influences Spanish, the main language. Added to this is lunfardo, a slang much loved by writers, humorists, and many porteños. It is said to have grown from life in the nineteenth-century portside slums and is heavily influenced by Italian and immigrant terms. Lunfardo is part of the porteño culture, with descriptions and dictionaries sold in local bookshops. There is even a Buenos Aires Lunfardo Academy with specialists who trace the roots of words and their meaning.

blonde hair, so they tend to think of themselves as the Europeans of Latin America. Whatever their coloring, the women of Buenos Aires are famed for their elegance. The 3 percent of darker-skinned porteños have come from either the Middle East or the Andean highlands in the northwest of the country. During the 1700s, as many as 50 percent of Argentina's population was black, but because of high death rates, the end of the slave trade, and the government's encouragement of white immigrants and discouragement of black, few Afro-Argentineans remain in Buenos Aires.

Minority Groups

Immigrants from Europe and the Middle East brought much diversity to Buenos Aires. Minority groups living in Buenos Aires include Muslims from Syria, Lebanon, and other Middle Eastern countries; they are known locally as *turcos*. Many flourish trading goods, from textiles to foods, and they have built a prominent mosque and Islamic Center in the Palermo district.

Early in the nineteenth century, Great Britain's foreign policy encouraged investment in Argentina. The late nineteenth and early twentieth centuries saw British influence at its greatest as the British developed ranches, railways, banking, and other businesses. The suburb of Hurlingham became a mirror of life in Great Britain, with its private schools, churches, clubs, and sports, including polo. The men worked in the city, while the women typically thrived in the suburbs or

enjoyed meeting friends in the city's fashionable tearooms. This way of life continues—although with far less excessive display of wealth than fifty years ago.

Other Europeans—Swiss, French, and Russians among them—helped create the charmingly ornate city. Some Japanese arrived in the later half of the 1800s and established themselves as expert dry cleaners and horticulturists, while the recent influx of Koreans, Chinese, and Japanese in the 1990s tend to specialize in retailing and small-scale manufacture of consumer goods. All are represented through cultural activities and in restaurants specializing in their country's cuisine.

The Historic Metropolitan Cathedral

The Metropolitan Cathedral (pictured above) is the most important Catholic church in the city. Since its foundation in 1580, it has been rebuilt and was not finished until 1827. The present building dates from 1745, although the neoclassical grand façade is from the French style of the early nineteenth century. The twelve columns represent the twelve apostles; the sculpture above by a French artist depicts the arrival of Jacob in Egypt. The cathedral also holds part of Argentineans' history, because within the quiet of a side chapel lies the grand tomb of General José de San Martín, who led the fight for independence from Spain.

"In many respects cosmopolitan Buenos Aires is a strange mixture. Its culture is mostly French and Italian; but, socially, England and the United States of America have had a great influence. . . . England is responsible for the introduction of sports and most games, where the United States of America has flooded Argentina with all that goes with films, motor-cars, jazz and swing music."

—A. F. Tschiffely in *This Way Southward*, 1940.

Religion

The Spaniards brought the Roman Catholic religion to the Plate River and Buenos Aires. About 90 percent of the population today considers itself Roman Catholic, although only about 20 percent attend church regularly. Their major holidays are Easter and Christmas.

The oldest surviving church is San Ignacio, built in the early 1700s; it stands at the corner of a narrow street in the Manzana de las Luces, part of the historic city center. Unfortunately, vibrations from traffic threaten its fine baroque front, and it has to be propped up.

The patron saint of the city is San Martín de Tours. Another popular saint is the saint of the poor, San Cayetano. On his feast day on August 7, thousands of porteños,

Cemetario de La Recoleta

The ultimate sign of success and wealth in Argentinean life is to be buried in the Cemetario de La Recoleta (pictured above). This cemetery is so densely occupied that it has been described as the most expensive plot of land in the world. Walking into the cemetery is like entering a miniature city, with streets lined with sculptures and huge mausoleums dedicated to the most famous Argentinean citizens. Eva Perón is buried here, although, curiously, her husband Juan Perón and the famous singer Carlos Gardel are not. They are buried in another enormous cemetery, La Chacarita, in the north of the city.

believing he can bring them prosperity, work, and peace, make a pilgrimage to the working-class district of Liniers to pay him respect at a sanctuary. The harsh economic years of the late 1990s and early present century saw the number of pilgrims increase dramatically.

Jewish Community

Argentina has the largest Jewish community in Latin America with over 300,000 members; more than 200,000 live in Buenos Aires. Most descended from immigrants from France, Germany, and Eastern Europe. Today, as in the past, the Jewish community is at the forefront of culture and politics in the city.

Most Jewish life is centered in the barrio of Once, home to Templo de la Congregación Israelita, Argentina's oldest synagogue. In recent years, however, the size of the community has been dwindling due to emigration and some anti-Jewish feeling. A terrorist bomb killed twenty-nine people at the Israeli Embassy in 1992, and another killed nearly ninety when a Jewish center was attacked in 1994. Hundreds were injured. Some Jews, especially young ones, have left because of the anti-Semitism these events have exposed.

Food

Probably no one meal can be said to be typically porteño. Sheep raised in the far south are served as the delicacy called Patagonian lamb, while the tropical north

▲ With marble columns and tiled floors, the Confiteria Violeta is typical of the grand tearooms and restaurants established in the city over a century ago.

offers many delicious fruits. The vineyards of the Andean foothills provide some of the finest wines in the world, many made by French or Italian producers..

Spanish immigrants from Galicia have their own favorite delicacies, including crispy roast suckling pig and fish. People of Italian ancestry favor noodles; the city offers more than two thousand pasta restaurants. Because it is believed to bring good luck, it is the custom to eat *nõquis*, or potato dumplings, on the 29th of each month.

Beef reigns supreme in cattle-raising Argentina. A traditional beef steak is served with bread and a salad, usually of tomatoes and onions. The most popular way that beef is cooked is on a barbecue, or *parrilla*. A traditional parrilla also includes many other cuts of meat, including sweetbreads, brains, and hearts.

Snacks and Treats

A snack can be *choripan*, a spicy chorizo sausage in a bread roll, or an *empanada*, a little fried or baked pastry packet filled with meat, cheese, or corn. Another popular snack is a *miga* sandwich, an Argentinean tradition that came with the British. The bread is thin and the fillings generous. Sometimes triple decked, migas contain ham, cheese, tomato, or other tasty items. While the *sandwich de miga* is available almost everywhere, no good tearoom is without an *alfajor*, or sweet-filled pastry cookie.

Yerba Mate: Jesuit's Tea

Ask an Argentinean to name a national drink, and the answer will be yerba mate *(pronounced mah-tay).* Mate *is a Native American name for the gourd or cup used to contain the drink, and* yerba *means "herb." Yerba mate comes from a short tree related to holly that has leaves containing a stimulant.*

In the seventeenth century, Jesuit missionaries found the local Native Americans using the dried leaves to make an infusion like tea. By 1645, they had begun commercial production. Traditionally, the finest mates are made of delicately beaten silver and the tea is sipped through bombillas, *or drinking straws, also of silver and exquisitely finished. At the everyday level, the mate is a simple gourd and the bombilla consists of a stainless steel tube.*

CHAPTER 3

Living in Buenos Aires

On arrival at the city's international airport, many people's first impression is of open space. This changes quickly during the hour-long drive to the center. Three times as many people live in the city proper, per square mile, compared with the number living in the suburbs.

Housing

The central part of city is compact, with long roads crossed by dozens of streets. As the older part grew in the nineteenth and through the twentieth century, space was left open in the form of parks or simple, tree-lined squares. Even in the heat of summer, these bring some relief and shade to the mass of brick and concrete.

In a block in one of the elegant areas such as Recoleta, many apartments have fine entrance halls with marble floors. Often the elevator will seem to be a relic, with brass handles and heavy accordion-like grille doors. In less wealthy parts, the apartments are simpler, although they often have small balconies where clothes can be dried or aired. Garages for cars may be underneath. Neighbors can see from one side of the street to the other. Life on the block usually

◄ *Brightly painted houses characterize La Boca, one of the city's oldest barrios, which is favored by artists.*

Street Names

Almost every street in Buenos Aires, especially in the center, has some historical reference. Many are named after politicians, presidents, and military men, such as Sarmiento, Belgrano, Lavalle, and San Martin. Others commemorate important historical events, such as Islas Malvinas, Defensa, Reconquista, Avenida 9 de Julio, and Plaza de Mayo, which commemorates May 25, 1810, when a gathering in the plaza called for independence from Spain. One street is named after Carlos Gardel, the tango singer, and another after the Spanish explorer Juan Diaz de Solis, who reached Rio de Plata in February 1516, landed, and was killed by Native Americans.

includes a small restaurant or snack bar for pastries or empanadas, where people meet for refreshment and relaxation.

Back in the late nineteenth century, wealthy ranchers, railway builders, and shipping families had fine homes in Buenos Aires, and many of these buildings still stand. In the city's historic Monserrat neighborhood, the Museo de la Ciudad, or the City's Museum, gives a glimpse of what life was like for a prosperous family of that time. The museum is set in the home of a nineteenth-century store owner's family. Electricity warms the bedrooms, the kitchen

▼ *Most Porteños live in apartments in high-rise buildings like these in Recoleta.*

contains a stove and enamelware, and a collection of family photographs shows the wedding customs and dress of the day.

The museum is above La Estrella, "The Star," an old drugstore that has also been kept in its original form. Rows of large glass jars remain from the days when medicines were made by hand according to doctors' orders. The jars still contain long-forgotten basic materials such as camphor, balsam, and various salts.

Today, the suburbs of Buenos Aires are filled with low, gray concrete houses set side by side. *Villas miserias*, poor shanty homes of recycled brick and sheet metal, have been built in the city. The government hopes to replace these with more substantial apartment blocks.

Recent years have brought some dramatic changes. Economic problems have left many people without money, so the villas miserias have grown, especially along railway lines and main roads. At the other extreme, spectacular high-rise apartments

▼ *Many homes in the villas miserias are made of cardboard and sheet metal. Often a family with several children sleeps in a one-room home.*

▲ *This spectacular building, erected in 1931 to house the Abasto market, is now a giant shopping mall.*

have been built overlooking the old port area with recreational facilities. The gap between rich and poor is growing: In 2001, over one-quarter of the population lived in poverty; today, that number is closer to half.

From Tiny Stores to Huge Malls

Shopping in Buenos Aires mixes traditional and new. The smaller, family-run shops in many of the suburbs supply food, clothes, and household items. Even in the city's center, these small stores have not disappeared entirely, although they are tucked away off the more expensive main streets. Tiny, often narrow shops opening directly onto the sidewalk sell drinks and snacks; many stay open late at night.

At the other extreme are new supermarkets and shopping malls. For example, Abasto Mall was converted from an old market place with an art deco front. It is now a modern mall with individual shops, restaurants, and a children's museum, all

San Telmo Market

On weekends, the city comes alive with small, mostly outdoor markets where people buy and sell odds and ends or curiosities. Of all these flea markets, the one in San Telmo is the most famous, drawing crowds of porteños and tourists. The flea market is in Dorrego Square, the second oldest square in the city. Old books, porcelain, phonographs, compact discs, old telephones, cameras, china dolls, lace, and pictures of all kinds cram its market stalls. Most shoppers only have to browse to find something antique.

▲ *El Ateneo bookstore is housed in an old theater where people can browse and sit and read while enjoying tea and pastries in a small café.*

connected by escalators. The museum is full of life-sized models intended for education as well as fun, such as a TV and radio studio and even a toilet bowl large enough for children to see how plumbing works. Once a center for livestock auctions, the Patio Bullrich in Recoleta is another sophisticated mall known for its expensive restaurants.

Calle Florida

Calle Florida, or Florida Street, is a pedestrian avenue with shops of all kinds, banks, street-side kiosks, restaurants, and tearooms such as the elegant Richmond with its leather-backed chairs. This bustling street is a magnet for tourists trying to find bargains in real leather. Fine suede jackets and skirts fill the windows. Shoe shops offer many bargains. One block at the western end is occupied by the Galerías Pacifico, which is another mall outstanding for its painted domed ceiling and luxury shops. It dates from the nineteenth century.

Books and Arts

The city is famed for its wide range of cultural opportunities in the arts. There are numerous bookshops, and most stock both foreign and locally produced books. One spectacular bookstore, El Ateneo, is housed

Jorge Luis Borges

Argentina's greatest writer is probably Jorge Luis Borges, who was born in Buenos Aires in 1899. The city government is justifiably proud of his fame and promotes a museum of his work. Jorge Borges spoke English before Spanish, thanks to the influence of his British grandmother. "Georgie," as he was known at home, began his career as an author by writing an outline of Greek mythology in English when he was six. From then on, he did not stop. He studied in France and wrote poems, essays, and short stories describing Buenos Aires and life in the shanties, the tango, and fights with knives. He received awards and went on to live in Switzerland, where he died in 1986.

in an old theater with its balconies crammed with volumes on different subjects. Buenos Aires has an annual international book fair and a modern National Library. Newspapers have a long history here, with the major daily *La Prensa* dating back to October 1869, when the first copies were published. An English-language newspaper, the *Buenos Aires Herald*, was founded only seven years later in 1876; today, both are available online.

Schools

All children in Argentina ages six to fifteen must attend school for a total of nine years. Public schools are free, but there are no public school buses and students must buy their own books. A school uniform usually consists of a white laboratory coat worn over everyday clothes. At private schools, uniforms may mean jackets and shorts for younger boys and colored skirts and blouses for girls.

For most students, one group of pupils starts school at eight and finishes at noon, then a second group begins at one and finishes at five. This is often the only way all students can receive lessons. The school year in Buenos Aires runs from early March until mid-July when there is a short break. School begins again at the end of July and continues until early December.

The day begins by raising the nation's flag and singing the national anthem. Set by the government, the curriculum includes classes in science and arts, subjects similar to those taught in the United States and Europe.

Higher Education

At fifteen, students have to choose one series of subjects they want to study at a university. There are five choices, including humanities and social sciences; natural sciences; economy and management; communication, art, and design; and production of goods and services, which includes electronics, chemistry, and architecture. For students who do not want an academic career, there are also vocational schools.

Buenos Aires has more than forty universities, including private universities

▲ Private school students work on a science project. Private schools, which families must pay for, often have better equipment than the public schools.

and two run by the Roman Catholic Church. The oldest, largest, and most widely respected is the state-run National University of Buenos Aires, founded in 1821, which has over 180,000 students, making it the largest university in South America. To attend, students must show they have completed high school but do not need other qualifications. Tuition is free, but only good students survive the lengthy courses, and relatively few eventually earn degrees.

CHAPTER 4

Buenos Aires at Work

A range of famous-name company buildings rises high above the newly developed waterfront in Buenos Aires. The scale and glittering design of these twenty-first-century icons is a clear statement that the city is the heart of Latin America's third largest economy.

Industry

Much of Argentina's industry is based in Buenos Aires; hundreds of companies have emerged from meat production alone. Workers produce packaging, labels, the meat-cutting machinery, clothing for the workers, and chemicals such as preservatives. At the consumer level, restaurants need equipment to grill the meat and plates and glasses to serve the meal. All these things are made in Argentina, and most of them in Buenos Aires.

The meat industry is just one part of the immense industry based on agriculture. Milk, butter, and cheese preparation and manufacturing packaging for fruit juices, soybeans, and oils are other parts of the city's industry. Tens of thousands of large and small companies contribute to the economy. Parts

◀ *Many corporate headquarters of Argentinean companies are housed in the newly built modern commercial center close to the port area.*

The Plate River has been vital to the economy of southern South American since Spanish times. The port of Buenos Aires is one of the largest in South America. When independent Argentina flourished, crossed by increasing numbers of trains, the old port was rebuilt and extended between 1909 and 1920. In 2003, ships arrived at the rate of five per day, and over 5.8 million tons (5.3 metric tons) of cargo was moved. Today, the port has been redeveloped for recreational activities. The latest docks, with facilities for huge ships carrying containers of goods, are nearby, close to the railway terminus.

for trucks and cars, elevators, kitchen and bathroom fittings, clothes, and leather goods come from factories in the suburbs. Many products are exported to other countries, providing income for Argentina as a whole.

Buenos Aires, the Movie Capital

Argentinean movie production is famed throughout the continent, and its latest young directors are winning praise around the world. Buenos Aires is the center of an industry offering dozens of producers, companies that rent and sell movie-making equipment, and postproduction facilities. The industry's beginnings came in the early days of silent cinema and then began to grow as sound films were created. The film *Tango*, released by Argentina Sono Film in 1933, was among the first movies filmed in Buenos Aires. Movie production continued throughout the bad economic times, and between 2000 and 2002, 137 films were released.

Today's brightest star director is Fabian Bielinski, whose thriller *Nueve Reinas*, "Nine Queens," is set around the story of a theft of rare stamps. The film has won seven Condor awards in Argentina and has been shown at the Museum of Modern Art in New York.

Getting around Buenos Aires

Traffic along the main city roads is mostly smooth running and fast; elsewhere it can be chaotic. Many taxi drivers seem to believe they are on a race car track and often race each other between the lights. Taxis are easily identified as they are painted black and yellow.

Buses fill the narrow streets in the older parts of the city. Approximately 2 million vehicles travel in the city streets daily, and the accident rate is much higher than for North American cities of similar size. Most people travel by bus or *colectivos*, microbuses that weave through the streets, picking up and dropping off passengers with amazing speed. As of 2004, the bus fare was just eighty cents to go anywhere in the city.

A subway system—the oldest in South America—of five lines runs to most parts of the city. It is known locally as the *Subte*, short for *subterraneo*. The lines are known by A, B, C, D, and E. With fourteen stations, the A line is the oldest, dating from 1913 to

▲ *Buenos Aires has a clean and efficient subway system that covers most of the city.*

1914. The subway cars on this line are the original carriages, with wood-framed interiors. About 12 percent of the city population travel to school or work by Subte, at a cost of seventy cents to any destination. Some stations are decorated to reflect the area they serve. For example, Carlos Gardel station on Line B is close to where this famous tango artist lived and is decorated with murals portraying him, and at the new station under the Cabildo, the platform displays sixteen busts of outstanding Argentinean personalities such as Jorge Luis Borges and Carlos Gardel.

Streetcar services were stopped in 1962, but one short line has been rescued by Friends of the Tramway, who run a service on weekends and holidays. The Friends use streetcars from Portugal or others found in derelict condition and now lovingly restored. Another old line has been renovated and equipped with new trains. It is known as the *Tren de la Costa*, "The Coast Train," and has a frequent daily service from the city, with eleven stops at tourist and weekend resorts along the edge of the Plate River.

Buenos Aires has an international airport, called Ministro Pistarini International Airport at Ezeiza, some 22 miles (35 km) south of the city, and the Aeroparque Jorge Newbery downtown, which serves other destinations in Argentina. A Buquebus, or hydrofoil, connects Buenos Aires to Colonia and Montevideo in Uruguay, with several daily trips.

National Government

Argentina ranks as the eighth largest country in the world with territory stretching from the tropics to the chill subantarctic. Within this huge land lie twenty-three provinces and the Federal District of the capital. While each province has its own elected governor, legislature, and judicial system, they are under the umbrella of the national government based in Buenos Aires. The president works at the Casa de Gobierno, "Government House," known locally as the Casa Rosada. An elected National Congress composed of a Senate and Chamber of Deputies sit in the Congresso Nacional, "National Congress," in the imposing Plaza de los dos Congresos. Serving six-year terms, seventy-two senators are elected, with each province and the Federal District represented by three senators. The Chamber of Deputies has 257 members who serve four-year terms.

▼ *The National Congress Building, inaugurated in 1906, contains one of the country's largest libraries.*

Mothers of the Disappeared Ones

A human rights group known as the "Mothers of the Plaza de Mayo" (pictured left) has held a protest every Thursday at 3:30 in the afternoon in the Plaza de Mayo for many years. The protestors are the mothers, and sometimes grandmothers, of sons, daughters, and other relatives who "disappeared" during the repressive regime of the military in the Dirty War of the 1970s and 1980s. They want the government to reveal its part in and information about the many thousands who were taken away by the government police for supposed political offences, never to be seen again.

Local Government

Run by the federal government from 1880 until 1996, Buenos Aires was the capital of Argentina when the city adopted the name and new constitution of *La Ciudad Autónoma de Buenos Aires,* "the Autonomous City of Buenos Aires." The constitution provides for a mayor and vice mayor along with sixty (amended now to seventy) representatives to govern the city. Signed on October 1, 1996, the constitution's aim is to promote development of the city and maintain equality, justice, and human rights for its citizens.

The elected mayor and vice mayor both remain in office for four years and can be re-elected for one further term. Between them,

they are responsible for ten government departments, ranging from city planning and education to culture and social development. Composed of elected deputies, the city's legislative office is headed by a president and three vice presidents.

In the metropolitan area of Buenos Aires, the basic political unit is the suburb, or *partido.* An elected mayor and municipal council govern each partido.

Economic Problems

For many years, Argentina seemed to enjoy the good life. Even the poorest levels of society had beef, bread, and wine, although often little more.

After years of troubles, the 1990s saw a short economic boom, then crash; the government's mismanagement, corruption, and overspending caused a huge international debt that could not be paid off. The government took drastic steps, including limiting the amount of money people could take from their bank accounts so it could keep what little the banks had. Waves of protest and panic spread through the country. In Buenos Aires, many bank buildings were attacked and branches closed. Huge demonstrations filled the streets, and thousands of people became poor overnight.

The existing villas miserias swelled with homeless, often formerly middle-class people. Scavenging through garbage became a new way of life, and children appeared on the streets sorting and collecting the garbage. They are known as the *cartoneros*, or collectors of cardboard, but they also gather together any other items that can be sold or recycled. At midnight, the downtown area of Buenos Aires comes alive with children collecting; each gang has its own area. They leave the garbage they cannot recycle in neat piles on any patch of grass they find.

Pollution

In spite of its economic troubles, however, the city remains relatively pollution free. Unlike some Latin American mega cities, the air of Buenos Aires is almost smog free in spite of the growth of industry. Pollution

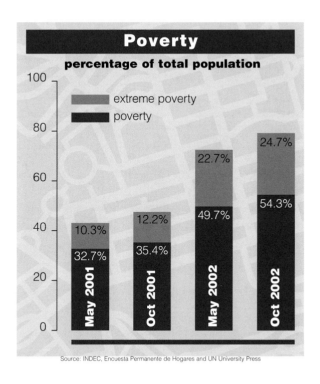

Poverty

percentage of total population

Source: INDEC, Encuesta Permanente de Hogares and UN University Press

▲ This chart shows the effect that the economic crash of late 2001 had on the people of Buenos Aires. Here, people living in households that cannot afford all basic needs—such as food, clothing, transportation, education, and health care—are counted as living in poverty. Some of them cannot even afford their basic food needs, and they are counted as living in extreme poverty.

levels can rise when the air is still, and a haze can be detected, but, for the most part, the winds from the Plate River estuary keep the city fresh.

Water pollution, on the other hand, is an issue, with manufacturing industries creating most of the problem. It is estimated that as much as 30 percent of the population of Buenos Aires drinks contaminated water.

CHAPTER 5

Buenos Aires at Play

Buenos Aires has safeguarded much of its heritage in museums. More than a hundred collections, large and small, include those contained in a Railway Museum, a Post and Telegraphs Museum, and an Automobile Collection. The city has huge collections of art and science and natural history exhibits.

Teatro Colón

One museum covering music, costumes, instruments, and photographs of performances and performers is housed in the Teatro Colón, or Colon Theater. Planned in 1829 and finished in 1908, this grand theater, one of the jewels of the city, is known throughout the world. The remarkably ornate interior with marble staircases, a painted ceiling, and a chandelier with six hundred lights has been the setting for hundreds of glittering performances. There is seating for twenty-five hundred and standing room for another one thousand. Many of the world's finest stars have set foot on the stage—opera singers Enrique Caruso, Maria Callas, Luciano Pavarotti, and Placido Domingo and ballet stars Rudolf Nureyev and Vaslav Nijinski among them.

◄ *Wildly enthusiastic fans of the famous soccer club the Boca Juniors fill the stands of the team's stadium, known as La Bombonera in November, 2002.*

Tango

The sound of Buenos Aires is the music of the tango. The history of tango dates from the late 1800s when it began as both a kind of music and a complex dance in the city's port slums. When the sons of wealthy Argentinean families traveled to Europe, they brought it to Paris; by 1913, the tango had become a worldwide phenomenon. The name comes from one given to the carnivals and dances of the nineteenth-century African community in Argentina. As that community declined, local whites and European immigrants retained parts of its tradition.

▲ *Tango shows take place in many bars and restaurants throughout Buenos Aires.*

A tango festival is held late February or early March in Buenos Aires when over 150 performers give free shows and concerts, followed by International Tango Week. A weeklong World Tango Festival featuring folk dances and music takes place in October with national and international dancers. December 11 is National Tango Day, when a week of celebrations revolves around the birthday of tango singer Carlos Gardel.

Carlos Gardel

For most Argentineans, the tango is inseparable from the life of Carlos Gardel who was born in France in 1890. Carlos and his mother separated from his father and immigrated to Buenos Aires when he was two years old. He spent his childhood near the Abasto Market, and in about 1912, he began his music career as a singer. A year later, Gardel teamed up with an Uruguayan, José Razzano, and they began singing duets, performing in many theaters in Argentina and Uruguay. By 1925, Razzano had given up singing, but he continued as Gardel's business manager for several more years.

Over the next ten years, Gardel traveled, making recordings of tango and other songs and giving performances in many famous venues in Latin America, Europe, and the United States He also sang in many films. In 1935, following a radio show in the Colombian capital Bogotá, he set out on a short flight to the city of Medellín, and his plane crashed. Gardel died and Argentina mourned its loss. In 2003, sixty-eight years after his death, a museum opened in a street near the Abasto Market in the house he bought in 1927 and where he lived with his mother until 1933.

Beyond the Tango

Always best known for the tango, Argentinean music has a far broader spectrum and appeal due to the population's diverse ethnic roots. Chamame music, popular in the northeastern region around Corrientes on the Parana River, stems from a mix of the culture of European immigrants, including Polish and Austrian, African music, and elements of the Quarani Indian tradition. Folk themes performed by stars like Mercedes Sosa and Atahualpa Yupanqui became the *nueva canción*, the "new song," of the 1960s and 1970s. Mercedes Sosa collaborated with composer Ariel Ramírez and Felix Luna to bring the ideas of the Spanish and Native past together in Cantata Sudamericana (South American Cantata). Rock first appeared in 1976 with MIA (Musicos Independientes Asociados), a cooperative of twenty-one people. Before one of their albums was even released, four thousand fans had sent in mail orders for it. To the present time, names such as Open Minds, Los Piojos, and Fun People have dominated the Argentinean music scene.

Soccer

Porteños are great soccer fans. The two best-known teams are the Boca Juniors, founded in 1905, and the River Plate, founded in 1901. Their rivalry is legendary; Boca Juniors regard themselves as "the people's team," while the River Plates are "the millionaires." River Plate fans are

"Football [soccer] is one of Argentina's most cultural activities."

—President Carlos Menem in 1999.

known to Boca fans as *gallinas* or "chickens," while River Plate fans call Boca fans *bosteros*, which comes from a word for horse manure. Each team has its own stadium. River Plate, which has won most championships locally, plays at the El Monumental stadium, while La Boca have their own stadium, La Bombonera, nicknamed "The Sweetbox." It holds over sixty thousand supporters.

La Boca is perhaps best known as the home team of one of the world's greatest

▲ *The British introduced polo to Argentina, where it was a great success. In 1924, the first Argentinean team to enter the Olympics won the gold medal.*

soccer players, Diego Maradona. He was born the fifth of eight children in 1960 in a poor district of Buenos Aires and made his international debut in 1977. By 1982, he was a well-established member of Argentina's national team, when he was hired first by a team in Barcelona, Spain, and then by the Italian club, Napoli.

Jorge Newbery, Argentinean Athlete

An idol of the early 1900s, Jorge Newbery was the son of an American father and Argentinean mother. He was an all-around sports star, with achievements in rowing, fencing, boxing, and wrestling. Owner of one of the city's first cars, he was a pioneer of auto racing. Newbery took up flying and was a founding member of the Argentinean Aero Club. In 1909, he broke the South American altitude record for flying in a balloon, followed by establishing a world altitude record piloting a monoplane. Soon afterward, however, he died in a crash in 1914 when taking off in an attempt to cross the rugged Andes Mountains. Crowds of admirers attended his funeral in Chacarita cemetery; for years afterward, his tomb attracted scores of visitors. Aeroparque Jorge Newbery is the downtown airport named after him.

Maradona was at his best in the 1980s, but after a loss against West Germany in the final of the 1990 World Cup, he went rapidly downhill. He failed drug tests and in 1997 retired from soccer to pass into the record books.

Other Sports

The city has two main racecourses with horseracing on virtually every day of the year. Polo is immensely popular, and major competitions are played on the city's grounds in Palermo. Argentina has won every world championship since 1949. Another sport, el pato, is similar to polo. It originated among the gauchos in colonial times, with players on horseback hurling the pato, or ball, rather than hitting it with mallets.

Said by many to be the world's greatest race-car driver, Juan Fangio won many races with spectacular skill, including the Formula One World Championship five times. From 1953 through 1957, Fangio thrilled crowds at the Autodromo race track in Buenos Aires, winning the Grand Prix of Argentina four times.

Recreation

One of the joys of living in Buenos Aires is the abundance of its open public spaces. Parks abound; fountains, landscaping, avenues of trees, and statues of the famous lend a feeling of tranquility even in the most troubled times. Children can play while families picnic; retirees sit on park benches reading newspapers. One space known as the Jardín Japonés (Japanese Garden)—a gift from the emperor of Japan—marks the one hundred-year anniversary of the arrival of the first Japanese immigrants to Buenos Aires. A red bridge, a Japanese pagoda-style restaurant, and a cultural center are set among flowering shrubs. It is located in the Palermo district alongside the Parque Tres de Febrero (February 3 Park), created by Charles Thays. Nearby stand the Botanical Gardens and the city's zoo.

▲ *Palermo is the most popular spot in the city for spending weekends and relaxing.*

The riverside offers more open space, and one area close to the old Puerto Madero, known as the Costanera Sur, has been set aside as an ecological reserve. Part swampland, the 890 acres (360 hectares) attract many waterbirds, especially migrating ones, and it has become a favorite place for walkers, cyclists, and birdwatchers. For the less energetic, the city is famous for sidewalk cafes and bars where people meet and enjoy the warmth of summer days. In winter, it can be cold in Buenos Aires, and life moves indoors.

Charles Thays

A landscape artist, Charles Thays was born in France in 1849 and settled in Argentina. He transformed many sterile, colonial plazas into tree-filled parks, reminiscent of London's Hyde Park or New York's Central Park. Among his best-known works in Buenos Aires are the Plaza San Martin, the Botanical Gardens that are named after him, and the Barrancas in the exclusive barrio of Belgrano, with trees, paths, and gardens with fountains and statues. Thays preferred a casual style of landscaping and used many local trees and shrubs such as the jacaranda, the palo borracho (the drunken tree), and small palms. He died in 1934.

CHAPTER 6

Looking Forward

The crippling economic years of the early twenty-first century have left scars on Buenos Aires, but from the time of its foundation, the city has always enjoyed a great momentum. Hope for the future lies with the porteños who have faced up to the reality of the bad times and are now rebuilding their lives at a surprising pace. The city is alive with creative ideas and has become a magnet for tourism. The port is busy and looks set to grow as trading increases between the countries of Argentina, Uruguay, Paraguay, and Chile. These countries, members of an organization called Mercosur, promote movement of goods, services, and people between their countries.

The Puerto Madero Development

When the thousands of immigrants arrived by sea at the end of the nineteenth century, they found a port that could have been part of the dock areas in New York City. The architect was Eduardo Madero, whose name is given to this port of four interconnected docks backed by low, red-brick warehouses. An imposing customs house that is still standing lies on the city side, while more warehouses and waste ground were nearer the Plate River.

Like many old docks around the world, The original *diques* (docks) in Puerto Madero

◄ *The redevelopment of Porto Madero has created a monument to the past and a beacon for the future.*

and their warehouses were falling into disuse as facilities for containerships opened in a new port nearby. The federal government decided to bring life back to the area, and the Antiguo Puerto Madero Corporation SA was formed in 1989 with the national government and city of Buenos Aires as equal partners. A national competition for a development plan drew many entries; once the winner was chosen, the work commenced.

A New Life for Old Docks

The old warehouses were gutted and converted into offices, a university, and restaurants. Stylish new office buildings, apartments, hotels, and a museum were built. A pedestrian bridge now spans the docks at one end while an extraordinary restaurant with a leaflike roof stands at the other. The docks are now a yacht harbor, and land has been reclaimed as a wildlife sanctuary. For anyone arriving in Buenos Aires, even after an absence of a few years, the skyline and feel of the area are unrecognizable. The old Puerto Madero, dating from the 1880s, has become the city's showpiece for the future.

Now Puerto Madero's population is growing, today numbering more than seven thousand, and by 2007 it could be thirteen thousand. On weekends, the place bustles with visitors and tourists. An intriguing new pedestrian bridge, the Puente de la Mujer (the Bridge of the Woman), has a central section 335 feet (102 m) long suspended from an inclined pylon 128 feet (39 m) high. This central section can be rotated to allow tall ships to pass.

On the way, ships pass one of the world's classic vessels for training people to sail, the *Presidente Sarmiento*, now a museum. Yachts and small, privately owned boats have taken over the docks, attracting more business. For the time being, the plan seems to be working.

A Promising Future

Unlike many Latin America cities, Buenos Aires has space to expand and extremely good connections with the rest of Argentina and neighboring countries. Many people still live in poverty, however, and a fundamental problem has been the shortage of energy. In July 2004, Argentina signed a treaty with neighboring Bolivia to import gas from that country. This, together with an improvement in agricultural exports, signals the return of an upbeat economy and a promising future not only for the people of Buenos Aires, but all Argentineans.

"Buenos Aires...may not be quite as much fun as Rio, and it certainly isn't as serious as New York or Mexico City; but nowhere in the entire Americas has as much style as Buenos Aires."

— John Simpson, BBC correspondent, 1996.

Time Line

2000 B.C Native Americans farm and settle into communities in the area of Buenos Aires.

A.D. 1516 Europeans first reach the Plate River, calling it the Río de la Plata.

1536 Pedro de Mendoza founds the first settlement; he also introduces the first cattle and horses.

1580 Juan de Garay founds the second, successful settlement and names it Nuestra Senõra Santa María del Buen Aire.

1667 Buenos Aires has about four thousand inhabitants.

1751 The Cabildo, or town hall, is constructed.

1776 The Spanish crown names Buenos Aires the capital of the Viceroyalty of Río de la Plata.

1806 British troops commanded by General William Beresford invade Buenos Aires.

1807 British troops under General John Whitelocke invade Buenos Aires again.

1810 Buenos Aires declares its independence from Spain.

1816 Argentina becomes a republic.

1821 National University of Buenos Aires is founded.

1829–52 Juan Manuel de Rosas is governor of Buenos Aires.

1869–1914 Population of Buenos Aires the grows from 177,000 to over 1 million with flood of immigrants from Europe.

1880 Buenos Aires becomes the capital of Argentina.

1880s General Julio Roca wipes out the last of the indigenous people in the south of the country.

1919 One thousand people are killed in protests during *la semana tragica*.

1940s The population of Buenos Aires reaches 5 million.

1946 Juan Perón becomes president.

1952 Eva Duarte de Perón dies from cancer.

1955 The military overthrows Juan Perón; Casa Rosada is bombed, and three hundred die during a protest; in retaliation, Peronists burn down many of the city's churches.

1970s Guerrilla groups terrorize Buenos Aires and the country.

1973 Juan Perón becomes president for the second time.

1976 The military seizes power again.

1976–83 The military arrests and murders political opponents during a period known as the Dirty War.

1982 The military government goes to war with Great Britain over the Falkland Islands.

1983 Democratic government is restored with election of President Raúl Alfonsín.

1989 Carlos Menem becomes president.

2003 Néstor Kirchner becomes president and helps stabilize the economy somewhat.

Glossary

anarchists people who follow the theory that all forms of government are oppressive and undesirable.

anti-Semitism prejudice against Jews or Judaism.

art deco an architectural and decorative style of 1925 to 1940 that uses bold outlines and geometric designs.

barrios neighborhoods or boroughs.

chorizo a dry and very spicy sausage made with pork.

colonial relating to a colony, a territory that is far away from the country that governs it.

contraband goods not allowed by law to be imported or exported; they are smuggled into a country.

estuary the mouth of a large river.

facade the outside front of a building.

gaucho a South American cattle herder of the pampas, similar to the North American cowboy.

Great Depression a period of economic hardship, from 1929 to 1939, when people around the world lost their jobs, homes, farms, and businesses.

immigrants people who move to a new country and settle there.

Jesuit a member of the Roman Catholic order called the Society of Jesus.

mausoleum a huge, magnificent tomb often constructed in marble.

nationalism devotion to the interests and culture of a particular nation.

obelisk a monument of stone tapering at the top like a pyramid.

pampas large and flat grassy plains.

patron saint a saint who is supposed to protect a place or organization and to whom that place or organization is dedicated.

pilgrimage usually a journey made for a religious purpose such as visiting a holy place.

porteño a person who lives in Buenos Aires.

Roman Catholic describes a Christian tradition of worship headed by the Pope in Rome.

sanctuary a sacred place or a reserved area where birds and other animals are protected from hunting.

street grid system a network of streets and avenues crossing at ninety-degree angles.

viceroyalty a large territory in the Spanish colonies governed by a viceroy who represented the Spanish king or queen.

villas miserias shantytowns where the poor of Buenos Aires live.

Further Information

Books

Bao, Sandra, and Ben Greensfielder, *Lonely Planet Buenos Aires*. Lonely Planet, 2002.

Bernhardson, Wayne, *Moon Handbooks Buenos Aires*. Avalon Travel Publishing, 2003.

Kent, Deborah, *Buenos Aires (Cities of the World)*. Children's Press, 1998.

Krull, Kathleen, *Lives of Extraordinary Women: Rulers, Rebels, (and What the Neighbors Thought)*. Raintree Steck-Vaughn, 2000.

Parker, Janice, *Political Leaders*. Crabtree Publishing, 1999.

Time Out Buenos Aires (Time Out Guides). Penguin Books, 2004.

Web sites

www.argentinesoccer.com
Find the scores, standings, and descriptions of important games in English on this Argentinean soccer Web site.

www.evitaperon.org
You can hear Eva Perón's voice and see her images on the Web site produced by her family.

www.geographia.com/argentina/buenosaires/Index.htm
For an introduction to Buenos Aires, its neighborhoods, and the surrounding countryside, check out this Web site and its links.

www.lonelyplanet.com/destinations/south_america/buenos_aires
This guide to the sights and sounds of Buenos Aires allows you to feel like a traveler in this exciting city and its surrounding area.

library.thinkquest.org/J002194F/mainpage.htm
Children put together this Web site on the tango and other Latin dances. It includes photos and short videos.

www.travelforkids.com/Funtodo/Argentina/buenosaires.htm
Discover fun things to do when visiting the city.

Index